DRESSING DOWNTON™

Changing Fashion *for* Changing Times

DRESSING DOWNTON™

Changing Fashion *for* Changing Times

TABLE *of* CONTENTS

FOREWORD

EXHIBITS DEVELOPMENT GROUP

It is with great pride that Exhibits Development Group (EDG), designer and producer of *Dressing Downton: Changing Fashion for Changing Times,* brings the exhibition to a worldwide audience with a premiere presentation at America's largest home, Biltmore Estate. Celebrating the success of the *Downton Abbey®* television series, this new exhibition brings to life the style and history of the beloved drama.

Adoring fans of this popular PBS program will have the chance to see the fashions of the Crawley family and their servants first-hand at North America's finest estate homes, museums and private institutions. Many of these beautiful buildings were constructed in the same period as depicted in *Downton Abbey,* which gives the venues the opportunity to promote their local histories.

EDG has curated and produced more than 50 exhibitions since its inception. In recent years, an increasing appetite among museum visitors for costume exhibitions has become evident, likely due to the popular appeal of period films and dramas like *Downton Abbey.*

This exhibition underscores EDG's commitment to bringing high-quality traveling exhibitions of art, science, history and popular culture to diverse audiences that promote international cultural exchange. It is with great pride that we share this project with you.

Amy Noble Seitz
Founder and CEO
Exhibits Development Group

COSPROP

The process of creating costumes for television and film begins when a film company contacts a costume designer. If the film calls for period costumes, that designer will more than likely turn to Cosprop for its unique qualities of unrivaled knowledge and unequaled workmanship.

This was certainly the case when *Downton Abbey*® first entered our collective consciousness. Cosprop was very much in demand for its fabulous collection of ready made and original period costumes as well as for its enviable museum of vintage costumes that offer inspiration and models for accurate reproduction.

On their first visit to Cosprop, designers express their requirements in detail using photographs, mood boards and script references. Costumes selected from stock are tried on the actors and lengths of fabric are used to establish both style and colour. An existing costume may be perfect for the role as it is; it may be remade to fit the actor; or it may be used as a starting point for creating a new garment. The actors participate in the deliberations. Some, such as Maggie Smith, have often been dressed at Cosprop – as Maggie was for *Downton Abbey*.

Supplying costumes for *Downton Abbey* has been a fascinating task for Cosprop, adapting to different designers, meeting the sometimes-exacting demands of actors and following the flow of the many unfolding stories. It has been equally fascinating to put the *Dressing Downton* exhibition together, choosing the costumes that best illustrate the changing fashions of the time and that best distil the essence of each character. We hope this exhibition draws you closer to some of your best-loved characters and also gives you insight into some of the work that goes on behind the scenes.

John Bright
Founder and Director
Cosprop Ltd., London

INTRODUCTION

The costumes in the exhibition *Dressing Downton: Changing Fashion for Changing Times* come from the wildly popular British period drama *Downton Abbey*, a co-production of Carnival Films and PBS's Masterpiece. The television series has won numerous prestigious awards and has been recognized for its outstanding costume design.

The exhibition and this catalogue explore fashions in Britain between 1912, the year the Titanic sank, and the early 1920s, the dawn of the Jazz Age. This period, marked particularly by the impact of World War I (1914-1918), saw great changes in people's lives and in the way they dressed.

As the series opens we meet the Crawleys, living in the fictional Yorkshire estate of Downton Abbey. We meet Lady Mary, the eldest daughter of the aristocratic family, and her sisters. Their days are spent preparing themselves for a successful marriage.

> Women like me don't have a life. We choose clothes and pay calls and work for charity and do the Season. But really we're stuck in a waiting room until we marry. - Lady Mary Crawley

Much of the Crawley women's time is taken up with their wardrobe – dressing for a succession of social engagements that fill their days. The clothes in *Dressing Downton* feature the fashions worn by aristocratic families alongside the uniforms of their servants. The costumes are inspired by old photographs, paintings, patterns and magazine pictures. Some costumes are largely original. Others are made from vintage fabrics by highly skilled dressmakers with stunning results. Most are supplied by the renowned London costume house, Cosprop Ltd.

By showing period costumes in historical context, *Dressing Downton* illustrates the progression of style in Britain from the bustles and corsets of the Dowager Countess to the liberating, French-style fashion choices of Lady Sybil; from white tie and tails for men – *de rigueur* for formal dinners – to the more relaxed, short dinner jacket with black tie. There is a costume for every activity and time of day in *Dressing Downton*.

FASHION
INFLUENCES

HAUTE COUTURE

Women in the Edwardian period embraced *haute couture* and new fashionable styles. American women, like the Countess of Grantham, were particularly attracted to the House of Worth, which was established by a British designer in Paris. Worth made beautiful, elaborate and very expensive clothes, which were immensely influential in the fashion world of their day.

ELIZABETH MCGOVERN AS CORA CRAWLEY, COUNTESS OF GRANTHAM
Downton Abbey, Season 1, 1913

Silk day dress and coat with black frogging and large brimmed silk hat with net overlay, flowers and ribbon detail, worn at the Downton Village Flower Show. The three-quarter-length coat became known as the "lampshade silhouette" and appears in the wardrobe of all the Downton women.

Costume courtesy of Cosprop

ELIZABETH MCGOVERN AS CORA CRAWLEY, THE COUNTESS OF GRANTHAM

Downton Abbey, Season 3, 1920

Silk evening dress with net overlay and beaded panel in front, worn at dinner in Scotland and on other occasions. The pointed hips of the skirt were called panniers, which in the 17th and 18th centuries extended the width of a dress at the hips in an exaggerated manner, and which became fashionable again in this modified form just after the end of World War I. A contemporary source commented that skirts "though skimpy round the hem are much ampler about the hips where they often have panniers, draperies or flat flounces."

Costume courtesy of Cosprop; Necklace of freshwater pearls and garnets courtesy of Sophie Millard Jewellery

ELIZABETH MCGOVERN AS CORA CRAWLEY, COUNTESS OF GRANTHAM

Downton Abbey, Season 2, 1916-1917

Beaded dress with velvet jacket, worn at the hospital's Charity Concert. The ivory silk center panel, beaded with glass diamonds, pearls and seed beads, is a rare piece of vintage fabric.

Clothes were made to last, so panels of dresses were often re-used; lace was cut-down for collars or cuffs; ribbons were re-used in hats or trimmings. The original fabric in the center panel of this dress had become very fragile from the weight of the beads pulling on the silk. It was restored by adding a layer of net backing to strengthen the fabric.

Costume courtesy of Cosprop; Gold necklace with hanging pearl pendants courtesy of Sophie Millard Jewellery

ORIENTALISM

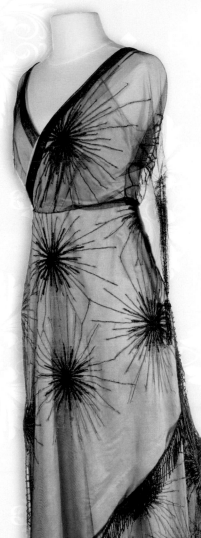

Fashion in pre-war Britain reflected the opulence of the period and a growing craze for all things oriental, partly sparked by a performance of "Scheherazade" in 1911 by Diaghilev's Ballets Russes. In fashion, Orientalism took many forms: pantaloons or "harem" pants as worn by Lady Sybil; exotic headdresses, including turbans; unusual shapes and beaded fringe as seen on Lady Mary. At the head of this movement was French designer Paul Poiret, who had trained at the house of Worth and was an apparent favorite of Lady Sybil.

MICHELLE DOCKERY
AS LADY MARY CRAWLEY
Downton Abbey, Season 1, 1913

Green silk evening dress, with black net overlay and black and silver starbursts, worn at dinner for Matthew's arrival at Downton. The style of this dress reflects the opulence of the pre-war period and the interest in Orientalism. The asymmetrical hem with beaded fringe is a typically exotic flourish.

Costume courtesy of Cosprop; Black jet beads courtesy of Sophie Millard Jewellery

ARTS & CRAFTS MOVEMENT

Lady Edith wears a coat that beautifully illustrates the Arts and Crafts movement. The style emerged in England during the late Victorian period, continuing its influence until the 1930s. It was an anti-industrial movement that valued handcraftsmanship and harked back to medieval, romantic or traditional folk styles of decoration.

LAURA CARMICHAEL
AS LADY EDITH CRAWLEY

Downton Abbey, Seasons 3-4, 1920–1921

An original coat, made of grosgrain edged in silk cannelle embroidery, first worn on a trip to London. This coat is a beautiful example of the influence of the Arts and Crafts style.

Costume courtesy of Cosprop

Designs of the Art Deco period (1909-1940s) are found in a number of Downton evening dresses – from the straight silhouette and geometric, diamond pattern of Lady Mary's silk and black net gown, to the sharp angles and geometric patterns of Martha Levinson's silk-velvet evening dress. Bakelite, an early plastic, was a popular material for Art Deco jewelry – as seen in the necklace Virginia Woolf wears to a London literary party.

MICHELLE DOCKERY
AS LADY MARY CRAWLEY
Downton Abbey, Season 2, 1917-1920

Dusty-pink silk evening dress with a black net overlay, creating a sheer and glamorous appearance enhanced by seed beads and sequins. The dress was worn at dinner the first time Sir Richard visits Downton. This beautiful dress has a less-defined waistline than earlier styles and marks the beginning of looser dress styles, which, as in this case, emphasized the wearer's slim figure. The straight silhouette and geometric diamond pattern hint at the Art Deco style, just coming into fashion at the time.

Costume courtesy of Cosprop; Long strand of clear glass beads with black accents courtesy of Sophie Millard Jewellery

SHIRLEY MACLAINE
AS MARTHA LEVINSON
Downton Abbey, Season 3, 1920

Evening dress of devour (or burnout) silk velvet in layers. The pattern in the outer layer is unmistakably Art Deco, with its sharp angles and geometric patterns. The front panel is embellished with black bugle beads. The dress was worn at the indoor picnic devised by Mrs. Levinson to save the day when disaster strikes the kitchen oven. For entertainment she serenades the Dowager Countess with a rendition of "Let Me Call You Sweetheart," a popular barbershop quartet song, first published in 1910 and first recorded by A Peerless Quartet.

→ *Costume courtesy of Cosprop; Necklace of emerald-like stones with rhinestone pendant courtesy of Sophie Millard Jewellery*

BOHEMIAN STYLE

Bohemian fashions reflected a yearning for an alternative lifestyle. We see this in Lady Sybil, who left her comfortable aristocratic upbringing to marry an Irish Catholic chauffeur with revolutionary political views. The influence of French Bohemian style is found in the medieval-looking embroidery on the hem and cuffs of Lady Sybil's maternity dress. The loose cut is also characteristically Bohemian, enabling the wearer to cast off her restrictive under garments.

**JESSICA BROWN FINDLAY
AS LADY SYBIL CRAWLEY**
Downton Abbey, Season 3, 1920

Velvet maternity dress with gold embroidered borders, worn first at dinner when Lady Sybil and Tom Branson return to Downton. The embroidery on the wide hem and cuffs is original and reflects the influence of a French Bohemian style on the aristocracy during this period.

By the early 1920s, the wartime need to economize on fabric coupled with women's more active lifestyles encouraged younger women to dress more adventurously. Many preferred the greater freedom that the looser silhouette and shorter hemlines allowed.

Costume courtesy of Cosprop; Long strand of glass beads in various shades of green courtesy of Sophie Millard Jewellery

CHRISTINA CARTY
AS VIRGINIA WOOLF
Downton Abbey, Season 4, 1922

Evening dress with a Bohemian feel and incorporating original fabric panels. The dress is worn at a London literary party that Edith attends with Mr. Gregson: it is glimpsed at the beginning of the scene, but the rest of the scene was left "on the cutting room floor."

The black silk-net fabric features intricate, metallic-thread embroidery known as Tambour work. This is characterized by rows of chain stitching worked with a hook on fabric held taut to resemble the head of a small drum, or tambour. The dress is stunningly set off by a necklace made of Bakelite, an early plastic that became a popular material for jewelry during the Art Deco period.

Costume courtesy of Cosprop; Necklace courtesy of Sophie Millard Jewellery

MEN'S FASHION

DAYTIME AND SPORTING STYLES

From the late Victorian period onwards, gentlemen on a country estate – and only on the estate – wore a tweed wool suit with calf-length beeches called "plus fours." Worn for daytime activities, plus fours, so-called because they were four inches longer than traditional knickers, were especially popular for hunting and other sporting activities such as cycling or walking. The choice for going into town, visiting neighbors or attending business meetings was a slightly more formal suit with long pants.

HUGH BONNEVILLE
AS ROBERT CRAWLEY,
EARL OF GRANTHAM
Downton Abbey, Season 1, 1913-1914

Light cream linen suit with straw Panama hat, often worn by the Earl of Grantham in the early years of the series starting with the Downton Village Flower Show. The pale color and light fabric of this suit echoes the heady, halcyon, carefree days of late-Edwardian Britain. The garden party scene, at which this suit also makes an appearance, has a light and airy mood, its characters unaware of the sadness of the war years to come.

⇥ *Costume courtesy of Cosprop*

HUGH BONNEVILLE AS ROBERT CRAWLEY, EARL OF GRANTHAM
Downton Abbey, Seasons 1-2, 1912-1920

A belted gentleman's suit, often worn with short boots and leather gaiters around the house and grounds of *Downton Abbey*. The wool fabric is warm and the cut is comfortable, except for the stiffly starched collar. Designer Caroline McCall commented that the male actors in *Downton Abbey* couldn't bear wearing the starched collar but did admit that as soon as they put them on they changed their posture and "went back in time."

Costume courtesy of Cosprop

IAIN GLEN
AS SIR RICHARD CARLISLE
Downton Abbey, Season 2, 1917-1920

Beautifully-tailored three-piece, wool herringbone suit; and wool coat, worn while walking with Lady Mary, Matthew and the family at Downton.

Self-made men like Sir Richard used their clothes to demonstrate their status: he wears expensive fabrics cut by the best London tailors. Dressed in wool for his country outing, Sir Richard complains to Lady Mary that he is feeling hot, prompting Mary to point out that he is wearing the wrong kind of fabric. Much to his embarrassment, while trying to fit into this grand country family, he has mistakenly ordered a heavy tweed suit – suitable for winter shooting but not for country walking.

⟶ *Costume courtesy of Cosprop*

EVENING FASHION

Evening clothes evolved from formal white tie and tails, to the more relaxed, short dinner jacket with black tie, very popular after World War I. The invention of white tie is widely accredited to Beau Brummell, an English dandy, who became the arbiter of men's fashion at the beginning of the 19th century. One of his many contributions to men's fashion was the simplification and codification of evening dress, whose essential elements – the monochromatic color scheme and ensemble of pants, coat, waistcoat and trousers – are still reflected in today's attire.

Although the use of white tie had been slowly in decline since the First World War, there has been a recent resurgence in interest, partially due to successful period dramas such as *Downton Abbey*.

DAN STEVENS
AS MATTHEW CRAWLEY
Downton Abbey, Seasons 1-3, 1913-1921

Known in the period as "White Tie," this formal outfit consists of a black tail suit with white or cream waistcoat, white shirt with detachable wing collar and white tie. The shoulders are rounder and softer than today's formal suits. This waistcoat is silk with pearl buttons. The trousers have a satin side-stripe. The shirt and collar are heavily starched and therefore very stiff. The separate collar (a mid-nineteenth century invention) was attached to the neckband of the shirt and held in place with studs. This made it easier to launder shirts as the collars could be starched separately. It also offered men greater choices in their dress as collars came in different styles.

Matthew often wears this evening suit and is wearing it at the Servants' Ball when he proposes to Lady Mary for the second time. After World War I, the short dinner jacket became an alternative choice for informal evening events and family dinners. But, the evening tailcoat remained standard wear for formal or ceremonial occasions.

→ *Costume courtesy of Cosprop*

GARY CARR
AS JACK ROSS
Downton Abbey, Season 4, 1922

Formal evening suit, as worn at the Lotus Jazz Club where Lady Rose hears Chicago-born Jack Ross singing the popular American song, "April Showers," a well-known Al Jolson trademark. Rose's invitation for the band to perform at Downton for Lord Grantham's birthday raises eyebrows both upstairs and downstairs: not only due to the color of Jack's skin but also to the new sounds of his jazz music.

Costume courtesy of Cosprop

DOWNSTAIRS FASHION

Servants' uniforms reflected tradition rather than fashion. They changed very little. Like contemporary lawyers, or clerks at chic dress shops, the Downton servants blended in, their clothes emphasizing continuity and reassurance. In the 18th century servants had dressed more individually, but by the 19th century dress had become more "uniform." The maid's uniform of black dress, white apron and white cap was a Victorian creation, designed to distinguish this group of servants from others. At Downton, the uniforms worn by male servants – footmen and the butler – do not change; the dresses of the housekeeper and lady's maids mirror changing fashions but always remain black.

PHYLLIS LOGAN
AS MRS. HUGHES
Downton Abbey, Season 1, 1913-1914

Working outfit of black silk and wool with cream lace trim. As the chief female servant, the Housekeeper dressed to emphasize her managerial status. Her clothes were always in somber colors and noticeably plain, except for the household keys, which hung from her waist. As a mark of respect housekeepers were always called "Mrs." regardless of whether they were married or not.

—❧ *Costume courtesy of Cosprop*

JOANNE FROGGATT
AS ANNA SMITH

AMY NUTTALL
AS ETHEL PARKS

ROSE LESLIE
AS GWEN DAWSON

CLARE CALBRAITH
AS JANE MOORSUM
Downton Abbey, Seasons 1-2, 1912-1919

Maid's black cotton dress with white lace trim on the sleeves and collar, and white cotton apron. Maids wore printed dresses and plain aprons for their morning cleaning duties. They changed into black dresses with decorative aprons, as here, for the rest of the day. As Head Housemaid and Lady's Maid, Anna is responsible for dressing the Crawley girls in the morning and again in the evening. Upper-class women usually dressed themselves for afternoon tea in what was called a "tea gown," a looser garment that could be worn without a corset. The Lady's Maid was also expected to care for clothes, fix hair and select jewelry, but not help with make-up as none was worn at the time.

Costume courtesy of Cosprop

ROBERT JAMES-COLLIER
AS THOMAS BARROW

THOMAS HOWES
AS WILLIAM MASON

ED SPELEERS
AS JAMES "JIMMY" KENT

MATT MILNE
AS ALFRED NUGENT

Downton Abbey, Seasons 1-4, 1912–1923

Footmen's uniform, or livery, was made from a wool and cotton fabric. At Downton, the footmen wore white ties and striped waistcoats with the family's crest on the buttons for their work upstairs. Below stairs, they covered their formal livery with an apron and sleeve protectors.

When a footman started in a big house he could be given a suit worn by previous footmen: but, if lucky, he was sent to the tailor to be measured for a new outfit. The footman was then responsible for keeping his own clothes clean and in good repair. Hired for their youth, height and good looks, footmen were called the "peacocks" of the household.

Costume courtesy of Cosprop

ALLEN LEECH
AS TOM BRANSON

Downton Abbey, Seasons 1-2, 1913-1918

The Chauffeur's uniform was based on a Victorian coachman's outfit. Although cars were less open to wind and rain than horse-drawn carriages, the drivers' uniforms still needed to be weatherproof. Overcoats were usually made from serge and lined with tweed for warmth: the double-breasted style also helped keep out the cold.

Coachmen traditionally wore top hats, but a chauffeur wore a peaked cap – with a chinstrap to secure it when driving at speed. Breeches and boots remained part of the uniform until the 1920s when cars became more enclosed and less draughty.

Uniform courtesy of Angels, The Costumiers

THE SHAPE OF FASHION

The clothes of the Dowager Countess of Grantham enhance her imperious nature and reflect the styles of Edwardian Britain, rather than the fashions of a younger generation. The shape of her early dresses is dictated by the costumes' under garments, particularly the S-bend corset, so-called because it accentuated the bosom, squeezed the figure in at the waist and pushed out at the back, somewhat like a Victorian bustle. The S-bend corset also helped carry the weight of a dress and its petticoats.

By 1912, dresses were becoming looser and shorter, with higher waists, thin belts and narrow skirts. Even though this style of dress appears to do away with the need for corsets, many were still worn with "stays." By 1914, the younger Crawley women favored a more modern, high-waisted type of corset – lightly boned and flexible but still able to straighten the silhouette.

It was the French designer Paul Poiret who created the corset-free, high-waisted dress, achieving something feminists and doctors had failed to do for years: liberate women from the corset. As corsets were abandoned so female body-shapes changed. By the time Lady Rose arrives on the scene in the early 1920s young women were embracing the brassiere rather than the corset, and were even binding their bosoms so that dresses and long necklaces hung correctly. Busts, waists and hips were no longer defined.

MAGGIE SMITH AS VIOLET CRAWLEY, DOWAGER COUNTESS OF GRANTHAM
Downton Abbey, Season 1, 1913-1914

This is the costume that sets the character of the Dowager Countess of Grantham. A staple of her wardrobe, this two-piece day dress appears many times in the early years of *Downton Abbey*. The fabric for the outfit, according to costume designer Susannah Buxton, was created by reproducing an Edwardian pattern. The design was based on a jacket from the era. Original lace was used for the edging and cuff detail. The silk bolero bodice is trimmed in black, set off with jewelry and a netted toque hat, a style made enduringly recognizable by Queen Mary.

Purple was chosen because the Dowager Countess is in half-mourning for family members killed in the Titanic disaster. Once an initial period of mourning was over, it was acceptable to wear colors such as purple, lilac or grey, as well as black.

Costume courtesy of Cosprop

LILY JAMES
AS LADY ROSE MACCLARE
Downton Abbey, Season 4, 1922-1923

Silk velvet evening dress, original to the period, with glass bead and sequin decoration, worn at supper and at an "At Home" party in London.

This evening dress is not full-length, as would have been the case before World War I. By the 1920s, stylish evening dresses were the same length as day dresses but straighter in style and looser in the bust. Lady Rose would probably not have worn a corset under this dress as young women were discovering the comforts of the less-restrictive brassiere. Although Rose denies being a Flapper, her style is moving in that direction.

Costume courtesy of Cosprop; Rhinestone jewelry courtesy of Sophie Millard Jewellery

TRIMMINGS & ACCESSORIES

Upper-class women wore fabrics of extraordinary richness, even during the day. Fabrics were trimmed with fine lace, beads, fur, delicate embroidery or eye-catching decoration. Accessories were equally important and social convention dictated what was worn when: jewels for the evening; a hat and small purse for going out; lace gloves for summer and soft kid leather gloves on colder days.

Lady Mary carries a handbag for travel, one that matches the velvet collar of her coat. Based on luggage styles, but smaller, the handbag soon became an essential accessory for working and traveling women.

Lady Mary's accessories also include a long necklace of jet, a black stone popular in the Victorian period and worn almost exclusively as a sign of mourning from the death of Albert, the Prince Consort, in 1861 to the death of Queen Victoria 40 years later. The jet industry died with the Queen but the fashion for long necklaces remained strong: women wore necklaces on all occasions – in cafes, at home, out for dinner, even on the beach.

SHIRLEY MACLAINE
AS MARTHA LEVINSON
Downton Abbey, Season 3, 1920

Martha arrives at Downton in a flamboyant car and an equally flamboyant coat made from a mixed silk fabric and beautifully trimmed with fox fur collar and cuffs. The coat is accessorized with a velvet purse with carved bone clasp and an embroidered hat decorated with pheasant feathers that have been curved and trimmed to show off their exotic pattern.

The bold, gold and black floral pattern, together with her showy fur collar and cuffs demonstrate that Martha has an American eye for fashion. Her flamboyant persona and Lady Grantham's reserved personality are reflected in their very different fashion choices. Even though Martha is an older woman she is more in tune with modernity than her daughter.

↠ *Coat courtesy of Cosprop*

MICHELLE DOCKERY
AS LADY MARY CRAWLEY
Downton Abbey, Season 1, 1913-1914

Evening dress worn at dinner the night of the hunt: the occasion when the Turkish diplomat appears with Mr. Napier and Matthew Crawley. Mary risks her chance of marrying well by entertaining the Turkish Diplomat in her room, where he suffers a heart attack in her bed.

Downton costume designer Susannah Buxton said, "This dress is made from a turn-of-the-century Spanish evening dress. We sourced beautiful silk chiffon and had it pleated for the cap sleeves and bands across the front. We built layers for the final effect, with embroidered lace laid over the deep-red satin under dress."

↬ *Costume courtesy of Cosprop; Garnet necklace courtesy of Sophie Millard Jewellery*

ELIZABETH MCGOVERN
AS CORA CRAWLEY,
COUNTESS OF GRANTHAM
Downton Abbey, Season 1, 1913

Excellent example of an ensemble complete with all the trimmings: silk day dress and coat with eye-catching black frogging, large-brimmed hat and a silk purse with silk tassels and white lace gloves.

 *Costume courtesy of Cosprop*

MICHELLE DOCKERY
AS LADY MARY CRAWLEY
Downton Abbey, Season 2, 1916-1918

Another complete ensemble for daytime wear: wool coat with velvet trim on the collar and cuffs; a felt hat with silk decoration; leather gloves; and a velvet handbag with a metal clasp. Once women came to rely on the handbag, there was no looking back: women have had one hand firmly on that bag ever since.

Costume courtesy of Cosprop

MAGGIE SMITH
AS VIOLET CRAWLEY,
DOWAGER COUNTESS
OF GRANTHAM

Downton Abbey, Season 3, 1920

Dress with an under layer of pale, olive-green satin and an overdress of black chiffon. The center panel shows a definite Japanese influence. The cuffs of the olive dress have original black, silver and white seed beading in a floral pattern with black and gold swirls. The dress was worn at the indoor picnic when the Dowager Countess is serenaded by Martha Levinson.

The silhouette of this gown is a real departure for the character of the Dowager. The elements of Edwardian dress that she will never give up – the high neckline and the corset – are still visible; but the S-bend shape is gone, giving her a more natural-looking waistline.

Costume courtesy of Cosprop; Necklace of pearls with rhinestone pendant courtesy of Sophie Millard Jewellery

The height of the use of accessories is on full display at the presentation ceremony for Lady Rose.

ELIZABETH MCGOVERN AS CORA CRAWLEY, COUNTESS OF GRANTHAM
Downton Abbey, Season 4, The London Season, 1923

The velvet, drop-waist, formal dress has original lace and beadwork from the 1920s on the bodice and sleeves, and is embellished with diamanté stones and gold seed beads. There is a sunburst pattern on the front and a simple train at the back. Worn with white gloves and a necklace of diamond-like stones.

This costume was worn by the Countess of Grantham as she accompanied Lady Rose on her presentation at Court before the King and Queen of England. The London ceremony was one of the most formal in the Royal calendar with an exceptionally strict dress code published by the Lord Chamberlain. Presenters had to wear a headdress of three, white Prince-of-Wales feathers attached to a tulle veil (Cora had her feathers and veil attached to a tiara and rhinestone hairpiece); a train (which could be either square or round ended); white or pale colored evening dress; and they had to carry a fan or bouquet. The form and measurements of dress were firmly stipulated.

→ *Costume courtesy of Cosprop; Jewelry courtesy of Sophie Millard Jewellery*

JANET MONTGOMERY
AS FREDA DUDLEY WARD

Downton Abbey, Season 4,
The London Season, 1923

Silk and silver beaded dress, worn to Lady Rose's Debutante ("Coming Out") Ball in London.

This dress is an outstanding example of 1920s' workmanship. The georgette layer with beading is original and has been strengthened by the addition of a fine net lining, to which the motifs are tacked. The satin underlay is wholly new, its slightly paler color brightening the look of the original georgette. The front panel is made from silver-accented lace, and the embellishments continue all the way around the dress. As with Lady Grantham's grey velvet dress, the beading on this gown has developed a patina that is impossible to achieve in recently made costumes.

When asked about using vintage costumes in the series, designer Caroline McCall said that during filming you could often hear the sound of loose beads dropping onto the floor.

POPPY DRAYTON
AS MADELEINE ALLSOPP

Downton Abbey, Season 4,
The London Season, 1923

Silk and silver beaded dress, worn to her and Lady Rose's Debutante ("Coming Out") Ball in London.

Debutante gown of silk satin with attached beaded panels. Worn by Madeleine Allsopp when she and Lady Rose are presented to the British Monarch. The gown is highlighted with a pearl headpiece and the requisite feathers and veil as well as a necklace of pearls and blue glass stones.

This gown was wholly made for the television series whereas the other two gowns worn to the Debutante Ball have elements original to the period. It is easy to see the difference in the patina of the beading. Sequins, beads and fringes became very popular in the 1920s as they showed off the dresses to their full effect as women moved across the dance floor. Dancers relished the upbeat sound of new dance crazes like the tango and the Charleston, and the 1920s became known as the "Roaring Twenties" or the "Jazz Age."

⟶ Costume courtesy of Cosprop; Pearl necklace with white and blue glass stones courtesy of Sophie Millard Jewellery

THE WAR & FASHION

During World War I fashions did not change, but clothes adapted to wartime conditions. Hemlines rose and stays were loosened after the Air Board commandeered the steel used for eyelets and requisitioned the machines that made them. The tailored suit was the most characteristic garment of the period. The women who wore such practical-looking clothes expressed their independence as they moved into the workforce and took up jobs outside the home.

MICHELLE DOCKERY
AS LADY MARY CRAWLEY

Downton Abbey, Season 2, 1916-1918

Wool coat with velvet trim on the collar and cuffs; a felt hat with silk trim; and a velvet handbag with a metal clasp, first worn on Mary's return trip from London where she meets Sir Richard Carlisle.

This two-piece ensemble is a practical style of dress, well suited to the war years. Tailored clothes for women, which derived from men's fashion, were worn for travel or sporting activities from the late 19th century onward. They came into their own during the war years, thanks to their practicality and economic use of fabric.

Costume courtesy of Cosprop

JESSICA BROWN FINDLAY
AS LADY SYBIL CRAWLEY
Downton Abbey, Season 1, 1913

Cotton and silk suit; straw hat with striped ribbon trim, worn for an afternoon outing of clothes shopping with the Countess of Grantham and Lady Edith. The three ladies were driven by Tom Branson, the chauffeur, who was later to become Lady Sybil's husband.

Costume courtesy of Cosprop

With men away fighting, women – even aristocratic women like Lady Edith – had to step into the workforce, undertaking every kind of job previously done by men. This often required women to wear traditionally masculine clothes such as breeches and trousers, something unheard of before the war. The experience gave many women a new confidence and sense of purpose. They realized that they could make a useful contribution to society in addition to getting married and raising children.

LAURA CARMICHAEL
AS LADY EDITH CRAWLEY
Downton Abbey, Season 2, 1917-1918

Wool cord breeches, brushed cotton blouse and linen jacket with contrasting velvet cuffs, lapels and waist belt: all cobbled together from Lady Edith's wardrobe for her work on the farm. Lady Edith had learned to drive the family car and volunteered to drive a tractor for a neighbor on his farm. The women who worked the land during the war were known as "Land Girls."

Costume courtesy of Cosprop

JESSICA BROWN FINDLAY
AS LADY SYBIL CRAWLEY

Downton Abbey, Season 2, 1916-1918

Nurse's cotton dress, apron and head scarf, as worn by Lady Sybil during the last two years of the war. The narrower silhouette and shorter skirt reflect wartime conditions: not only were fabric supplies limited, but shorter skirts for nurses avoided the problem of soiling from mud and blood on the floor.

Like many young women, Lady Sybil became a nurse in order to help the war effort. The new recruits tended men with terrible wounds and worked hard with little time to eat or sleep. The newcomers were not always welcomed by the trained nurses they worked alongside, but the huge numbers of wounded soldiers rendered their contribution invaluable.

Costume courtesy of Cosprop

MICHELLE DOCKERY
AS LADY MARY CRAWLEY
Downton Abbey, Season 2, 1916-1918

Crepe skirt and satin scoop neck blouse, incorporating original floral chiffon fabric for the front panel and cuffs, a simple style in keeping with daytime fashion seen during the First World War.

This ensemble is worn at the concert for convalescing soldiers, which is dramatically interrupted when Matthew and William appear: they had been assumed to be "missing-in-action." Matthew joins Lady Mary in singing a heartfelt rendition of "If You Were the Only Girl (in the World)," a popular song published in 1916 and introduced at the premiere of the London musical revue "The Bing Boys Are Here."

 *Costume courtesy of Cosprop*

MASS PRODUCTION

As an officer, Matthew Crawley would have had his uniform made by his own tailor. But the vast number of uniforms needed for ordinary soldiers led to garment-production methods being streamlined during the war. These new methods continued to be used after the war to mass-produce ready-made civilian clothing at lower cost and cheaper price. The impact on ordinary people's dress was enormous.

DAN STEVENS
AS MATTHEW CRAWLEY
Downton Abbey, Season 2, 1916-1918

Captain's wool uniform from World War I, worn throughout Matthew's war service and when he returns to Downton injured after the Battle of the Somme.

Uniform courtesy of Angels, The Costumiers

HUGH BONNEVILLE AS ROBERT CRAWLEY, EARL OF GRANTHAM

DAN STEVENS AS MATTHEW CRAWLEY

Downton Abbey, Season 2, 1916

Dress (Mess) uniform with red jacket, worn at the Charity Concert for the Hospital.

The military regiments featured in *Downton* are inventions: "The North Riding Volunteers" for the Earl of Grantham and "The Duke of Manchester's Own" for Matthew. Their crests and regimental badges are fictional, but based on authentic examples. The gentlemen's Mess Uniform (an outfit traditionally worn for meals in the officers' mess) was based on a 1912 Indian Guides officer's uniform.

Uniform courtesy of Angels, The Costumiers

THE BOYISH LOOK

After the war, Lady Edith fell for the latest fashion: the "boyish look." This precursor to the Flapper style, with dropped waist, raised hem and flattened bust, was achieved by wrapping bandeaux around the chest. Both Lady Edith and Lady Rose wear evening dresses that are the same length as day dresses, but straighter in style and looser in the bust. As the youngest lady in the Grantham household, Lady Rose embraces the new styles, new music and the latest dances, sometimes moving outside acceptable norms and adopting some of the relaxed behavior of the 1920s' Flapper.

LAURA CARMICHAEL
AS LADY EDITH CRAWLEY
Downton Abbey, Season 3, 1920

Evening dress made of two layers of silk: the top layer of sheer, shot chiffon has a gold iridescent quality. The drape at the drop waist is embellished with beaded embroidery and ribbons, as is the scooped neckline. The dress was worn at the indoor picnic and again in London. Lady Edith's dress is very much "of the moment." The thin straps, bare arms and neckline indicate that Edith's underpinnings are minimal.

⟶ *Costume courtesy of Cosprop*

TOUR SCHEDULE

Biltmore
Asheville, North Carolina
February 2015 - May 2015

....

Paine Art Center and Gardens
Oshkosh, Wisconsin
June 2015 - September 2015

....

Virginia Historical Society
Richmond, Virginia
October 2015 - January 2016

....

The Richard H. Driehaus Museum
Chicago, Illinois
February 2016 - May 2016

....

Taft Museum of Art
Cincinnati, Ohio
July 2016 - September 2016

....

The History Museum
South Bend, Indiana
October 2016 - January 2017

....

Muzeo
Anaheim, California
February 2017 - May 2017

....

Cheekwood Botanical Garden and Museum of Art
Nashville, Tennessee
June 2017 - September 2017

ACKNOWLEDGMENTS

The making of an exhibition is no small feat – it takes a collaborative effort requiring specialists from around the world. Most notably, Diane Salisbury deserves special recognition for her work as curator of and project director for *Dressing Downton: Changing Fashion for Changing Times*. This exhibition is the third costume exhibition developed by Ms. Salisbury, who has served as EDG's Director of Exhibitions, leading its curatorial and development team in artistic and cultural projects. A pioneer in the traveling exhibition field, Ms. Salisbury developed countless exhibitions ranging from antiquities and fine art to popular culture over the last 40 years. We salute her in this commemorative publication.

Exhibit Development Group would like to thank the following for their support in bringing *Dressing Downton: Changing Fashion for Changing Times* to fruition:

Cosprop Ltd.

Costumier

John Bright
Bernard Chapman
Christine McSweeney

Angels, The Costumlers

Costume Designers

Susannah Buxton
Rosaline Ebbutt
Caroline McCall

Sophie Millard Jewellery

NBCUniversal

Downton Abbey licensor and producer

Dominic Burns
Nick Young

Museum of London

Dr. Cathy Ross

Exhibits Development Group

Exhibition Producer

Amy Noble Seitz
Diane C. Salisbury
Jessica Grandbois
Elizabeth Frerichs
Carrie Reid

Geoffrey M. Curley + Associates

Award winning theater and exhibition designers

Geoffrey Curley
Eric Hugunin
Dave and Kathy Monk

Nancy Lawson

Costume Specialist and curator